Oxford REVISE

EDEXCEL GCSE

HISTORY

The American West, c1835–c1895

COMPLETE REVISION AND PRACTICE

Series Editor: Aaron Wilkes

James Ball

OXFORD
UNIVERSITY PRESS

Contents

 Shade in each level of the circle as you feel more confident and ready for your exam.

This book uses the term Indigenous peoples and Indigenous nations, as well as Native Americans. Many of the 5.5 million Indigenous people in North America today use these terms, as well as others, including the term Indian and Indians, which you will see in sources and interpretations in this book. Usually, though, Indigenous people talk about their identity in terms of their nation or tribe, such as the Cherokee Nation.

How to use this book

This book uses a three-step approach to revision: **Knowledge**, **Retrieval**, and **Practice**.
It is important that you do all three; they work together to make your revision effective.

Knowledge comes first. Each chapter starts with a **Knowledge Organiser**. These are clear easy-to-understand, concise summaries of the content that you need to know for your exam. The information is organised to show how one idea flows into the next so you can learn how everything is tied together, rather than lots of disconnected facts.

Answers and Glossary

You can scan the QR code at any time to access sample answers, mark schemes for all the exam-style questions, a glossary containing definitions of the key terms, as well as further revision support go.oup.com/OR/GCSE/Ed/Hist/AmWest

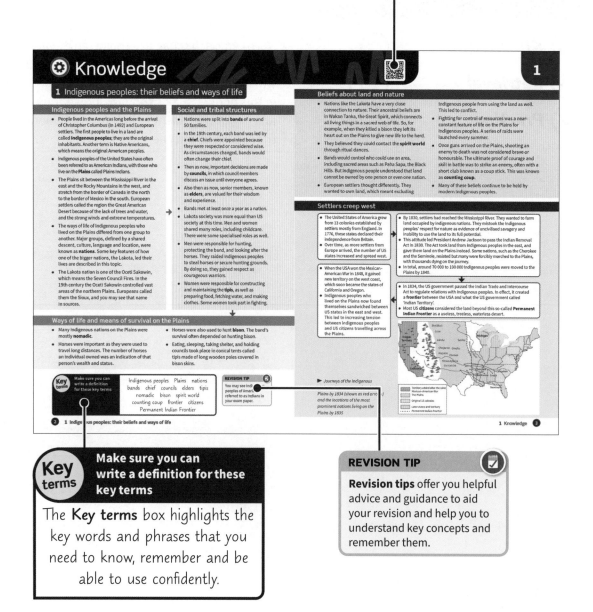

Key terms
Make sure you can write a definition for these key terms

The **Key terms** box highlights the key words and phrases that you need to know, remember and be able to use confidently.

REVISION TIP

Revision tips offer you helpful advice and guidance to aid your revision and help you to understand key concepts and remember them.

Retrieval

The **Retrieval questions** help you learn and quickly recall the information you've acquired. These are short questions and answers about the content in the Knowledge Organiser you have just reviewed. Cover up the answers with some paper and write down as many answers as you can from memory. Check back to the Knowledge Organiser for any you got wrong, then cover the answers and attempt all the questions again until you can answer *all* the questions correctly.

Make sure you revisit the Retrieval questions on different days to help them stick in your memory. You need to write down the answers each time, or say them out loud, otherwise it won't work.

Previous questions

Each chapter also has some **Retrieval questions** from **previous chapters**. Answer these to see if you can remember the content from the earlier chapters. If you get the answers wrong, go back and do the Retrieval questions for the earlier chapters again.

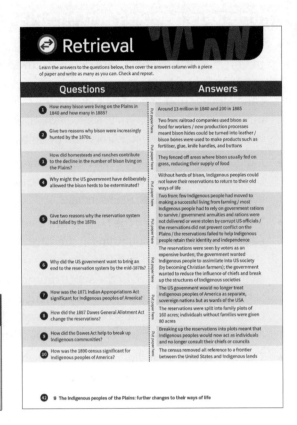

Practice

Once you think you know the Knowledge Organiser and Retrieval answers really well, you can move on to the final stage: **Practice**.

Each chapter has **Exam-style Questions**, including some questions from previous chapters, to help you apply all the knowledge you have learnt and can retrieve.

EXAM TIP

Exam tips show you how to interpret the questions, provide guidance on how to answer them, and advice on how to secure as many marks as possible. Guidance is also offered on how to approach different command words.

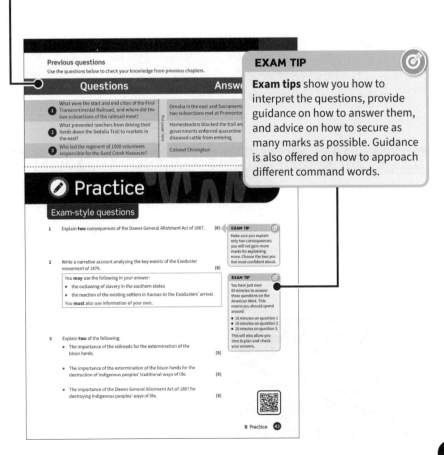

⚙ Knowledge

1 Indigenous peoples: their beliefs and ways of life

Indigenous peoples and the Plains

- People lived in the Americas long before the arrival of Christopher Columbus (in 1492) and European settlers. The first people to live in a land are called **Indigenous peoples**; they are the original inhabitants. Another term is Native Americans, which means the original American peoples.

- Indigenous peoples of the United States have often been referred to as American Indians, with those who live on the **Plains** called Plains Indians.

- The Plains sit between the Mississippi River in the east and the Rocky Mountains in the west, and stretch from the border of Canada in the north to the border of Mexico in the south. European settlers called the region the Great American Desert because of the lack of trees and water, and the strong winds and extreme temperatures.

- The ways of life of Indigenous peoples who lived on the Plains differed from one group to another. Major groups, defined by a shared descent, culture, language, and location, were known as **nations**. Some key features of how one of the bigger nations, the Lakota, led their lives are described in this topic.

- The Lakota nation is one of the Oceti Sakowin, which means the Seven Council Fires. In the 19th century, the Oceti Sakowin controlled vast areas of the northern Plains. Europeans called them the Sioux, and you may see that name in sources.

Social and tribal structures

- Nations were split into **bands** of around 50 families.

- In the 19th century, each band was led by a **chief**. Chiefs were appointed because they were respected or considered wise. As circumstances changed, bands would often change their chief.

- Then as now, important decisions are made by **councils**, in which council members discuss an issue until everyone agrees.

- Also then as now, senior members, known as **elders**, are valued for their wisdom and experience.

- Bands met at least once a year as a nation.

- Lakota society was more equal than US society at this time. Men and women shared many roles, including childcare. There were some specialised roles as well.

- Men were responsible for hunting, protecting the band, and looking after the horses. They raided Indigenous peoples to steal horses or secure hunting grounds. By doing so, they gained respect as courageous warriors.

- Women were responsible for constructing and maintaining the **tipis**, as well as preparing food, fetching water, and making clothes. Some women took part in fighting.

Ways of life and means of survival on the Plains

- Many Indigenous nations on the Plains were mostly **nomadic**.

- Horses were important as they were used to travel long distances. The number of horses an individual owned was an indication of that person's wealth and status.

- Horses were also used to hunt **bison**. The band's survival often depended on hunting bison.

- Eating, sleeping, taking shelter, and holding councils took place in conical tents called tipis made of long wooden poles covered in bison skins.

Key terms

Make sure you can write a definition for these key terms

Indigenous peoples   Plains   nation
band   chief   council   elder   tipi
nomadic   bison   spirit world
counting coup   frontier   citizen
Permanent Indian Frontier

REVISION TIP

You may see Indigenous peoples of America referred to as Indians in your exam paper.

Beliefs about land and nature

- Nations like the Lakota have a very close connection to nature. Their ancestral beliefs are in Wakan Tanka, the Great Spirit, which connects all living things in a sacred web of life. So, for example, when they killed a bison they left its heart out on the Plains to give new life to the herd.

- They believed they could contact the **spirit world** through ritual dances.

- Bands would control who could use an area, including sacred areas such as Paha Sapa, the Black Hills. But Indigenous people understood that land cannot be owned by one person or even one nation.

- European settlers thought differently. They wanted to own land, which meant excluding Indigenous people from using the land as well. This led to conflict.

- Fighting for control of resources was a near-constant feature of life on the Plains for Indigenous peoples. A series of raids were launched every summer.

- Once guns arrived on the Plains, shooting an enemy to death was not considered brave or honourable. The ultimate proof of courage and skill in battle was to strike an enemy, often with a short club known as a coup stick. This was known as **counting coup**.

Settlers creep west

- The United States of America grew from 13 colonies established by settlers mostly from England. In 1776, these states declared their independence from Britain.
- Over time, as more settlers from Europe arrived, the number of US states increased and spread west.

- By 1830, settlers had reached the Mississippi River. They wanted to farm land occupied by Indigenous nations. They mistook the Indigenous peoples' respect for nature as evidence of uncivilised savagery and inability to use the land to its full potential.
- This attitude led President Andrew Jackson to pass the Indian Removal Act in 1830. The Act took land from Indigenous peoples in the east, and gave them land on the Plains instead. Some nations, such as the Cherokee and the Seminole, resisted but many were forcibly marched to the Plains, with thousands dying on the journey.
- In total, around 70 000 to 100 000 Indigenous peoples were moved to the Plains by 1840.

- When the USA won the Mexican–American War in 1848, it gained new territory on the west coast, which soon became the states of California and Oregon.
- Indigenous peoples who lived on the Plains now found themselves sandwiched between US states in the east and west. This led to increasing tension between Indigenous peoples and US citizens travelling across the Plains.

- In 1834, the US government passed the Indian Trade and Intercourse Act to regulate relations with Indigenous peoples. In effect, it created a **frontier** between the USA and what the US government called 'Indian Territory'.
- Most US **citizens** considered the land beyond this so-called **Permanent Indian Frontier** as a useless, treeless, waterless desert.

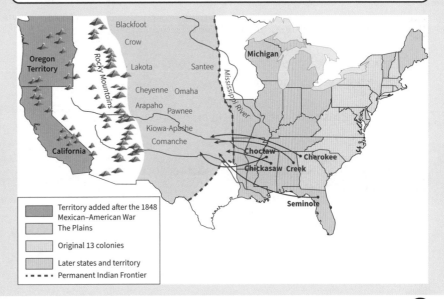

▶ *Journeys of the Indigenous nations who were moved to the Plains by 1834 (shown as arrows) and the locations of the most prominent nations living on the Plains by 1835*

Retrieval

Learn the answers to the questions below, then cover the answers column with a piece of paper and write as many as you can. Check and repeat.

	Questions	Answers
1	Define the term 'Indigenous peoples'.	The first peoples to live in a land
2	List two features of a tipi.	Made from long wooden poles covered in bison hides; used for eating, sleeping, taking shelter, and holding councils
3	List two features of the social structures of Indigenous peoples living on the Plains.	Two from: nations were split into bands of around 50 families led by a chief / chiefs were appointed because they were respected or considered wise / important decisions were made by councils / bands met as a nation at least once a year / men were responsible for hunting and protecting the band / women were responsible for the tipis and preparing food
4	Give two reasons why horses were so important to Indigenous peoples living on the Plains.	They were used to travel long distances; they were used to hunt bison
5	Why were bison so important to Indigenous peoples living on the Plains?	They relied on hunting bison for their survival
6	Why did many Indigenous peoples of the Plains leave the heart of a bison out on the Plains after killing it?	To give new life to the herd
7	How did Indigenous peoples such as the Lakota view the land?	Land could not be owned by an individual; nations had places that were sacred to them
8	What was counting coup?	Gaining honour in battle by striking an enemy with a short club called a coup stick
9	By which Act did the US government move many Indigenous peoples from the lands where they were living to the Plains?	1830 Indian Removal Act
10	Name a nation moved under this Act.	One from: Cherokee / Chickasaw / Choctaw / Creek / Seminole
11	How many Indigenous people were forced to leave their land under this Act?	Around 70 000 to 100 000
12	Why did President Andrew Jackson pass this Act?	Because people from the USA wanted to take the Indigenous people's land for themselves – they believed they could make better use of it
13	How did the USA gain the west coast territory of California?	By winning the 1848 Mexican–American War

Put paper here

Exam-style questions

1   Explain **two** consequences of the Indian Removal Act of 1830. **(8)**

2   Write a narrative account analysing the key events leading up to the establishment of the Permanent Indian Frontier. **(8)**

> You **may** use the following in your answer:
> - the westward spread of States
> - 1830 Indian Removal Act
>
> You **must** also use information of your own.

3   Explain **two** of the following:

- The importance of the US victory in the Mexican–American War for increasing tension between settlers and Indigenous peoples living on the Plains. **(8)**

- The importance of the horse to the ways of life of Indigenous peoples living on the Plains. **(8)**

- The importance of different attitudes towards land for tensions between Indigenous peoples and settlers. **(8)**

2 Migration and early settlement

Reasons for migration

Many US citizens migrated west in the mid-nineteenth century. Some felt forced to do so by difficult circumstances ('push factors'), while others were drawn by the idea of a new life ('pull factors').

Push factors	Pull factors	Manifest Destiny
<ul><li>In 1837, many banks and businesses failed due to an **economic depression** in the eastern states. Many people lost their jobs.</li><li>The arrival of large numbers of European **migrants**, particularly from Germany and Ireland, led to **overpopulation** and a shortage of land in the east. For example, the population of Missouri grew from 14 000 in 1830 to 343 000 in 1840.</li><li>Overcrowding and poor sanitary conditions led to outbreaks of cholera and yellow fever.</li></ul>	<ul><li>California and Oregon offered the prospect of fertile land, adventure, and freedom.</li><li>The discovery of a safe route through the Rocky Mountains in 1836 made the journey easier. This route became known as the **Oregon Trail**.</li><li>In 1841, the US government passed the Pre-emption Act. This allowed settlers to buy up to 160 acres of land cheaply before it was offered to anyone else.</li><li>The discovery of gold in California in 1848 triggered a Gold Rush in 1849.</li></ul>	<ul><li>Many US citizens saw it as their God-given right to seek out and claim free land for themselves, and to populate all of North America.</li><li>They believed it was their Christian duty to spread 'progress' and their 'superior' way of life.</li><li>This belief was known as **Manifest Destiny**.</li></ul>

The Gold Rush of 1849

- John Sutter discovered gold in California in 1848 whilst constructing a watermill.
- News of the discovery spread rapidly. The following year, 80 000 people arrived in California to seek their fortune. By 1853, there were 250 000 people looking for gold.
- Many thousands of people looking for gold made the hazardous journey across the Plains and over the Rocky Mountains, whilst others came by sea, including over 20 000 Chinese migrants.

The tough trails west

- The Oregon Trail was over 3200 km long. The combined length of the Oregon Trail and the **California Trail** was over 3800 km. The people who travelled on these trails in the 1840s and 1850s became known as **pioneer**
- The wooden carts that the pioneers travelled in were just three metres long and one metre wide. They were pulled by horses or oxen and coulc travel up to 20 km in a day. A typical journey lasted around 8 months and took place between April and November.
- Pioneers set off in groups called wagon trains, which included people with a variety of skills, including blacksmiths, hunters, and bakers, to help them survive the long and hazardous journey.
- Guidebooks were sold to help the pioneers, but the journey was still very hazardous. Sandstorms, snowstorms, torrential rain, swollen rivers quicksand, stampeding bison and cholera, were just some of the danger the pioneers faced.
- It is estimated that 34 000 men, women, and children died on the trails between 1840 and 1860. That's around 9 people for every kilometre of the Oregon Trail and the California Trail.

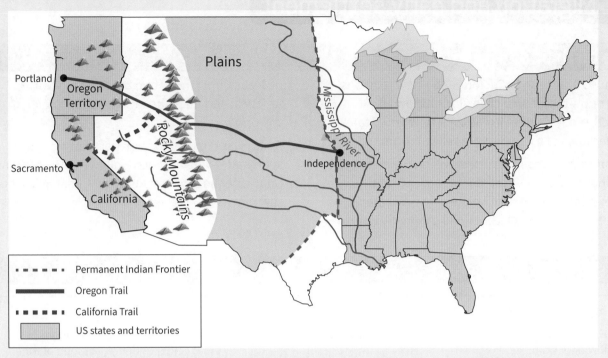

▲ *A map showing the Oregon Trail and the California Trail*

The Donner Party disaster

The disastrous expedition west led by the brothers George and Jacob Donner is the most infamous of all the pioneer journeys.

Mistakes	Consequences
• The wagon train containing the Donner Party left Independence in Missouri in May 1846. This was considered late in the year to leave.	• Conditions in the Sierra Nevada camp quickly became terrible. Animals froze to death, food ran out, and the pioneers faced starvation.
• The wagon train split into two groups when it reached Little Sandy River, about 1600 km from Independence. Around 80 people joined the Donner brothers and left the established trail to take a shortcut. None of them had travelled the new trail before and they found it blocked by boulders and tree roots. This made progress slow and dangerous.	• A group of 15 adults, including two Indigenous guides, set off to get help. Four of them soon perished. The others survived by roasting and eating the dead. The Indigenous guides, who refused to eat human flesh, also died and were eaten. After 32 days, the survivors finally found help.
• When deep snow fell as they tried to cross the Sierra Nevada mountains in October 1846, the Donner Party decided to stay where they were and make camp for the winter.	• Rescue parties were sent to find the camp in the Sierra Nevada. When the camp was discovered, those still living had also resorted to cannibalism to survive.
	• Fewer than 50 of the 80-strong Donner Party who took the shortcut made it to California.

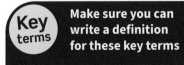

Key terms

Make sure you can write a definition for these key terms

Oregon Trail   Manifest Destiny   economic depression
migrant   overpopulation   California Trail
pioneers   Mormon   persecuted   irrigation

⚙ Knowledge

2 Migration and early settlement

The birth of a religion

- In 1820, Joseph Smith founded a new religious group – the Church of Jesus Christ and the Latter-day Saints – in Palmyra, New York State. Members of this group are called **Mormons**.

- Smith believed he had been visited by an angel, who told him the location of some ancient texts inscribed on gold plates. He translated the writings, which contained prophetic visions of Jesus Christ living and preaching in North America, and published them as *The Book of Mormon*.

- Smith was charismatic and persuasive, and soon had several hundred followers. His growing popularity angered mainstream Christians, who saw him as a blasphemous fraud.

Persecution in the east

From New York to Ohio

- Following an attack, the Mormons left Palmyra and settled in Kirtland, Ohio.
- The Mormons thrived in Kirtland and, by 1831, the community had over 1000 members.

From Ohio to Missouri

- In Kirtland, Mormons soon outnumbered non-Mormons, who began to resent Smith and his followers. They wrongly blamed the Mormons for the economic depression of 1837 and chased them out of town.
- The Mormon community headed for Missouri.

Trouble in Missouri

- The arrival of the Mormons in Independence, Missouri alarmed settlers already living there, who rioted in response. The army was sent in to restore order.
- Mormon leaders, including Smith, were blamed for the riot, imprisoned, and sentenced to death.
- They were eventually released on condition that they leave Missouri.

Increasing unpopularity of Joseph Smith

- In 1844, Smith claimed God had told him some Mormon men were allowed to have more than one wife. This caused great upset among both non-Mormons and also some Mormons, who did not believe a man should marry multiple women. The upset turned to outrage for some when they learned that Smith was planning to run to become President of the USA.
- On 27 June 1845, Smith was shot dead by an angry mob and Mormons were hunted down and attacked in the countryside.

To Commerce, Illinois – renamed Nauvoo

- Unwilling to go west into the Great American Desert of the Plains, Smith took the Mormons east to a tiny town called Commerce in Illinois.
- There, the Mormons worked hard and prospered, renaming the town Nauvoo (from the Hebrew word for 'beautiful place') and building a huge temple.
- By 1840, there were 35 000 Mormons in Nauvoo, with more converts constantly arriving from Europe.

The Mormon mass migration west (1846–47)

The new leader of the Mormons, Brigham Young, was a practical man and a brilliant organiser. He argued that as long as Mormons lived alongside non-Mormon US citizens they would always be **persecuted**.

Young decided to lead the Mormon community west, across the Plains, to the Great Salt Lake. He said, 'If there is a place on this earth that nobody wants, that's the place I'm looking for.'

- Moving 16 000 Mormons 2250 km across the Plains and over the Rocky Mountains to establish a thriving city seemed an impossible task. The first winter was spent building wagons, collecting provisions, and buying oxen.

- The Mormons divided themselves into a series of separate wagon trains, each containing 100 wagons under the control of a captain. Each wagon train was then subdivided into 'tens', each supervised by its own leader. This meant there was never any confusion over who was in charge.

- The first wagon train, which contained Young, stopped to build rest camps for those following. At every camp, people stayed behind to plant crops and build workshops for blacksmiths and carpenters.

- When Young's wagon train reached the Missouri River in June 1846, it stopped to build Winter Quarters – an encampment containing a thousand cabins in which all the Mormons could shelter throughout the freezing winter months.

- In April 1847, Young set off with a handpicked 'pioneer band' of 143 men, three women, and two children to lead the way to the Great Salt Lake. Here, they founded a settlement that was soon to become Salt Lake City.

- Young allocated land for each family to work and **irrigation** channels were dug to provide water. The pioneers' hard work and discipline meant the city thrived and many thousands more joined them.

The challenges of settling and farming on the Plains

Not all pioneers from the east travelled the whole way to the west. Some decided to stop and settle on the Plains. However, there they were met with a host of challenges.

Previously unfarmed soil was thick with tangled grass roots and quickly broke ploughs.

Grasshopper swarms destroyed crops.

Lack of trees meant that houses had to be made from earth (sod houses), and crops and animals could not be enclosed or protected by fences.

The challenges faced by pioneers settling and farming on the Plains

Prairie fires were common because of dry grass, lightning strikes, and violent winds (which fanned the flames).

Very hot, dry summers were followed by very cold winters.

The lack of rainfall meant it was a struggle to irrigate crops and provide enough water for both people and animals to drink.

Retrieval

Learn the answers to the questions below, then cover the answers column with a piece of paper and write as many as you can. Check and repeat.

	Questions		Answers
1	List two things that occurred in the east that 'pushed' settlers west.	Put paper here	Two from: economic depression in 1837 / overpopulation and shortage of land / outbreaks of cholera and yellow fever
2	List two things that 'pulled' settlers west.	Put paper here	Two from: the promise of fertile farmland, freedom, and adventure / discovery of the Oregon Trail / 1841 Pre-emption Act allowed settlers to buy land cheaply / gold discovered in California in 1848
3	What was Manifest Destiny?	Put paper here	The idea among US citizens that it was their God-given right to seek out and occupy all of North America; they believed it was their Christian duty to spread 'progress' and their 'superior' way of life by settling across the entire continent
4	How many people had travelled to California by 1853 during the Gold Rush?	Put paper here	250 000
5	Define the term 'pioneer'.	Put paper here	US citizens, either from Europe or descended from Europeans, who travelled west on trails across the Plains in the 1840s and 1850s
6	Approximately how many pioneers died on the Oregon and California trails between 1840 and 1860?	Put paper here	34 000
7	Give two reasons why the Donner Party's journey ended in disaster.	Put paper here	Two from: the party set off late in the year / it took an unknown shortcut / it decided to camp in the Sierra Nevada for the winter
8	Who was the first leader of the Mormons and who took over from him after his death?	Put paper here	Joseph Smith; Brigham Young
9	Why did the Mormons decide to migrate across the Plains?	Put paper here	They experienced repeated persecution when they lived alongside non-Mormons
10	What factors led to the success of the Mormon migration to the Great Salt Lake?	Put paper here	Planning, organisation, discipline, leadership, and hard work
11	List three reasons why settling on the Plains was so difficult.	Put paper here	Three from: hot and dry summers and very cold winters / prairie fires / grasshoppers destroyed crops / low rainfall and lack of surface water / lack of trees to build houses and fences / previously unfarmed soil was thick with grass roots and broke ploughs

Previous questions

Use the questions below to check your knowledge from previous chapters.

Questions	Answers
1 Explain how Indigenous tribes and bands made decisions.	Each band was led by an appointed chief and big decisions were made by councils
2 How did Indigenous peoples living in North America view their lands?	Land could not be owned by an individual; nations had places that were sacred to them
3 By which Act did the US government move Indigenous peoples from their ancestral lands to the Plains?	1830 Indian Removal Act

Put paper here

Practice

Exam-style questions

1 Explain **two** consequences of Indigenous peoples of the Plains owning large numbers of horses. **(8)**

EXAM TIP

On the exam paper, you will be given separate spaces to describe each consequence. Make sure you use both spaces and don't write about both consequences in one space.

2 Write a narrative account analysing the key events that led to the Donner Party disaster in 1846. **(8)**

You **may** use the following in your answer:

- arrival at Little Sandy River
- setting up camp in the Sierra Nevada

You **must** also use information of your own.

EXAM TIP

The question contains two bullet points, which you can use as the focus for your first two paragraphs. Remember that you must also include information of your own though. Come up with a third idea and write it on the question paper to remind you to write a third paragraph.

3 Explain **two** of the following:

- The importance of the discovery of gold in California for the increase in the number of US citizens migrating west. **(8)**

- The importance of Joseph Smith's declaration that it was permissible for some Mormon men to have more than one wife for causing the establishment of Salt Lake City. **(8)**

- The importance of the climate for the struggles that pioneers experienced when settling on the Plains. **(8)**

Knowledge

3 Early settlement: conflict and tension

Reasons for increased conflict on the Plains

- In the 1840s, a growing number of settlers moved both onto and through the Plains.
- The Gold Rush of 1849 meant the number of migrants crossing the Permanent Indian Frontier onto the Plains increased dramatically.

- The movements of the great herds of bison, which Indigenous peoples relied on, were disrupted by the arrival of huge numbers of settlers on the Plains.
- The increase in the number of settlers also scared other wild animals away, making it more difficult for Indigenous peoples to hunt.
- With a shortage of bison and other animals to hunt, Indigenous peoples increasingly took to raiding other tribes for scarce resources.

Both Indigenous people and migrant settlers asked the US government to intervene:

- Indigenous peoples wanted the government to safeguard the natural resources on which they depended.
- Settlers wanted the government to protect them from attack as they travelled west across the Plains.

In 1851, the government passed the Indian Appropriations Act.

- The sight of Indigenous peoples often caused the migrant wagon trains to panic and assume they were under attack.
- This often led to bloodshed and increasing levels of mistrust and hostility on the Plains.

The 1851 Indian Appropriations Act

- The Permanent Indian Frontier had created a border between the land that the US government wanted and land that it considered uninhabitable. The land to the west of the frontier was, therefore, left to Indigenous peoples to do with as they wanted.

- The Indian Appropriations Act marked an end to this way of thinking. The Act set aside government money to be used to encourage Indigenous peoples to move to, and stay in, specific areas of the Plains, known as **reservations**.

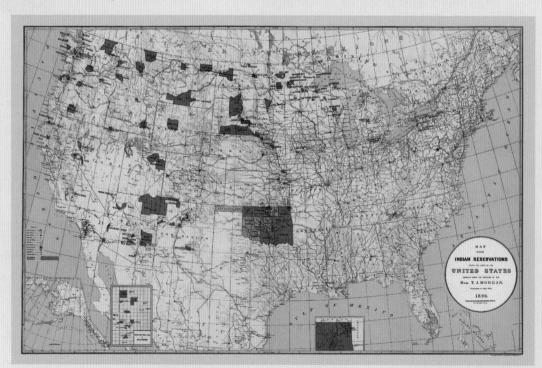

▶ *The coloured areas on this map indicate the land set aside for reservations in 1890. The size of the reservations in 1890 were much smaller than when they had been established in 1851*

The 1851 Fort Laramie Treaty

The government used the first available funds from the Indian Appropriations Act to establish the Fort Laramie Treaty of 1851.

Members of the Arapaho, Cheyenne, Crow, and Sioux nations met with the US government at Fort Laramie.

The Treaty attempted to:

- reduce conflict between Indigenous peoples and US migrants and settlers
- increase the safety of settlers moving across the Plains.

Indigenous nations agreed to:	US government agreed to:
☑ Live and stay in a specific territory (reservation) set out in the treaty to reduce contact and conflict between Indigenous peoples and US migrants. ☑ Allow the government to build roads and military forts along the trails that crossed the Plains and allow railroad surveyors safe access.	☑ Ensure that the land promised to Indigenous nations in the Treaty would belong to them permanently. ☑ Give Indigenous nations $50 000 worth of food and goods every year for 50 years.

Consequences of the 1851 Fort Laramie Treaty

- The Plains were no longer 'one big reservation' for all Indigenous nations. Each nation now had its own territory and access to the Plains was now guaranteed to settlers. The Permanent Indian Frontier no longer existed.

- The US army now patrolled the trails, which made the route feel safer and, as a result, the number of settlers passing across and settling on the Plains increased.

- Restricting Indigenous peoples to one area and hemming them in with roads and forts threatened their nomadic way of life.

- The structure of Indigenous society meant there was no equivalent of a US President who was in overall control and could negotiate and agree treaties on behalf of the whole Indigenous population. This meant many Indigenous peoples did not feel the Fort Laramie Treaty applied to them, as they had played no role in agreeing to it. Many more didn't even know the Treaty existed.

- As a result, when the US government did little or nothing to prevent its citizens from moving onto reservation land, despite what it had promised in the Fort Laramie Treaty of 1851, some people within Indigenous nations argued for war in order to drive the settlers off their land.

- Receiving annual government payments reduced Indigenous nations' independence. The US government could threaten to withhold the payments to control Indigenous peoples' behaviour. This increased calls within Plains nations for resistance against these threats to their existence as independent nations.

- The US government used any incident of Indigenous bands hunting outside their areas or raiding settler wagon trains as evidence that the whole nation was not meeting its Treaty obligations. And yet the US government rarely acted to uphold its own side of the Treaty of 1851. This increased hostility and resentment.

Knowledge

3 Early settlement: conflict and tension

Reasons for lawlessness in early towns and settlements

The new settlements established by settlers in the west experienced high levels of violence and other types of **lawlessness**. There were several reasons for this.

Claim jumping: This was a major problem in mining communities. **Claim jumpers** would assert ownership of other people's land if gold was discovered on it. **Miners' courts** sometimes helped settle disputes over a claim, but **cases** often ended in violence.

Population growth: The population of new settlements grew very quickly. For example, San Francisco's population grew from 14 000 in 1848 to 225 000 in 1852. Law enforcement and the **federal government** struggled to cope.

Lack of family stability: Most of the people who migrated west in search of gold were men who came without their families. Heavy drinking and gambling were common.

Guns: Most people carried a gun, so arguments swiftly escalated into gunfights.

Reasons for lawlessness

Criminals: Criminals were attracted west by the promise of 'getting rich quick' by tricking newly wealthy people out of their money.

Geography: The area that the US government had to police was vast and many mining communities were extremely isolated. People often took the law into their own hands before the authorities could act.

Unemployment: Only a tiny percentage of those who flocked to San Francisco became rich mining for gold. Far more commonly, fortune hunters became unemployed and turned to crime to survive.

Racial tensions: The discovery of gold attracted people from all over the world. Many white Americans believed they were racially superior and, therefore, more entitled to the gold. Racial tension often turned violent, with Chinese settlers in particular experiencing significant discrimination.

 Key terms
Make sure you can write a definition for these key terms

reservation   lawlessness
claim jumpers   miners' court
cases   federal government
US marshal   deputy marshal   sheriff
town marshal   vigilante   claim

REVISION TIP

Including specialist terminology in your exam answers is key to ensuring you are awarded high marks. Understand these key terms and use them at every opportunity.

Government responses to lawlessness

- The federal government was responsible for law and order in a territory before it became a state. They struggled to do this for several reasons.

- Some territories, such as California, were vast and were thousands of kilometres from the government in Washington.

- The federal government appointed US marshals, who then appointed deputies, to uphold the law in the territories.

- The marshals were poorly paid, many were corrupt and were too small in number to effectively police a territory the size of California.

US marshals were appointed by the President to maintain law and order in territories, which did not have their own law enforcement officials.

Deputy marshals were appointed by US marshals to help them cover the enormous areas. They were often appointed to specific towns or regions.

Sheriffs and town marshals were appointed by townspeople. They dealt with local issues such as saloon brawls and could appoint deputies as well as summon people to form a posse (group) to chase down criminals.

Local responses to lawlessness

San Francisco vigilantes

- When law enforcement officials struggled to cope with the level of crime, local residents sometimes took the law into their own hands.

- During the Gold Rush, San Francisco was in the grip of criminal gangs who murdered and stole, and bribed law enforcement officials at will.

- In 1851, concerned citizens set up a vigilance committee. The **vigilantes** took on the gangs, held their own trials outside of the law, and sentenced those found guilty to punishments such as deportation, whipping, or death by hanging.

Miners' courts

- The idea of vigilance committees soon spread to the mining settlements, where claim jumping disputes were common.

- Unofficial courts were set up, with a respected miner-appointed judge to decide who had ownership over a **claim**.

- In practice, the judgments reached were rarely fair and often depended on the ethnic background of the claimant. Chinese miners were specifically discriminated against and banned from working new claims.

Retrieval

Learn the answers to the questions below, then cover the answers column with a piece of paper and write as many as you can. Check and repeat.

Questions | Answers

1 Why did increased migration across the Plains by non-Indigenous people lead to increased raiding among Indigenous nations of the Plains?

The non-Indigenous migrants caused more scarcity of resources – fewer bison and other animals to hunt

2 What was the Permanent Indian Frontier?

A border between the settled land in the east and the land left to Indigenous peoples of America

3 What three things did representatives of Indigenous nations agree to in the Fort Laramie Treaty of 1851?

To live in specific reservations; to allow the government to build roads and forts on the Plains; to provide railroad surveyors and law-abiding travellers with safe access to their reservations

4 What two things did the US government agree to in the Fort Laramie Treaty of 1851?

Indigenous nations would own the reservation land permanently; the US government would give Indigenous nations $50 000 worth of food and goods every year for 50 years

5 Why did some Indigenous peoples believe receiving money from the government was a bad thing?

It could lead to loss of independence, as the government could threaten to withhold payment unless the Indigenous peoples did what the government wanted

6 Name three things that caused crime among settlers in the west.

Two from: claim jumping / rapid population growth / widespread gun ownership / difficulty of policing large areas / lack of family stability / opportunities to trick people out of their money / unemployment

7 How did racism lead to increased lawlessness?

Many white settlers believed they were superior to people of other races and more entitled to gold, which led to discrimination and violence

8 Name two types of law enforcement official.

Two from: US marshal / deputy marshal / town marshal / sheriff

9 What was a posse?

A group summoned to chase down criminals

10 Which city set up a vigilance committee in 1851 and what was the reason for it?

San Francisco; to control criminal gangs when law enforcement officials struggled to cope

11 Which ethnic group was specifically discriminated against by the miners' courts?

Chinese

Put paper here

Previous questions

Use the questions below to check your knowledge from previous chapters.

Questions	Answers

1 List two features of a tipi.

Made from long wooden poles covered in bison hides; used for eating, sleeping, taking shelter, and holding councils

2 What was Manifest Destiny?

The idea among US citizens that it was their God-given right to seek out and claim free land for themselves, and to populate all areas of the North American continent; they believed it was their Christian duty to spread 'progress' and their 'superior' way of life by settling across the entire continent

3 List three reasons why settling on the Plains was so difficult.

Three from: hot and dry summers and very cold winters / prairie fires / grasshoppers destroyed crops / low rainfall and lack of surface water / lack of trees to build houses and fences / previously unfarmed soil was thick with grass roots and broke ploughs

Put paper here

Put paper here

✎ Practice

Exam-style questions

1 Explain **two** consequences of the increase in settlers crossing the Plains after 1849. **(8)**

EXAM TIP

You are being asked about the consequences of the event in the question, so you should not write about the event itself. Focus on what happened as a result of the event.

2 Write a narrative account analysing the key events of the Mormon migrations between 1820 and 1847. **(8)**

> You **may** use the following in your answer:
> - leaving Kirtland
> - the death of Joseph Smith
>
> You **must** also use information of your own.

EXAM TIP

These questions ask you to identify the importance of the event, person, or development to the focus of the question. Use phrases like, 'This was very important because…', 'This was quite important as it meant…'.

3 Explain **two** of the following:

- The importance of the 1851 Indian Appropriations Act for improving the relationship between Indigenous peoples living on the Plains and settlers moving westwards. **(8)**

- The importance of the 1851 Fort Laramie Treaty for increasing hostility and resentment between Indigenous Americans and US migrants and settlers. **(8)**

- The importance of government responses for a reduction in lawlessness in the new settlements in the west. **(8)**

⚙ Knowledge

4 The development of settlement in the west

The impact of the American Civil War

The **American Civil War** (1861–65) had a big impact on the history of the west.

- Before the war, the states could not agree on how to settle the west.
  - Southern states wanted **plantations** (enormous farms) worked by enslaved African Americans.
  - Northern states had banned slavery and wanted thousands of small, family-owned farms in the west.
- Both sides wanted a railroad that ran west from their states.

- When the southern states seceded from (left) the USA and formed a new, unauthorised republic called the **Confederate States of America**, the Civil War started.
- The northern states (the Union) were now free to start settling the west how they wanted without the southern states voting against their policies.
- The war and Union victory in 1865 shaped how the west was settled.

The 1862 Homestead Act

The 1862 Homestead Act encouraged families to set up small farms and stopped rich people from buying huge areas of land.

To claim a **homestead** (160 acres of land), you simply had to:

- pay $10 (meaning most US citizens could afford to do it)
- be the head of a family or over 21. Immigrants, women, and formerly enslaved people could claim a homestead. Indigenous people and Confederate soldiers could not
- work the land for 5 years and then pay $30 to '**prove up**' the claim – i.e., make it permanent. Only one claim could be filed per person.

The Homestead Act: success or failure?

Successes:
- ☑ The Act encouraged many thousands of Europeans to travel to the US and settle on the Plains (although this led to further hemming in of Indigenous peoples).
- ☑ Homesteaders took up 6 million acres of the Plains by 1876 and 80 million acres by 1930.

Failures:
- ☒ Farming the Plains remained difficult, meaning that 60% of homesteaders never 'proved up' their claims.

Solutions to problems faced by homesteaders

Lack of water	Lack of trees	Hard, dry soil entangled with roots	Isolation
<ul><li>Additional water sources were often found when planting new land.</li><li>Lack of water was solved by new drills and wind pumps that drew water from deep underground.</li></ul>	<ul><li>The invention of barbed wire in 1874 enabled homesteaders to build fences without wood.</li><li>The Timber Culture Act of 1873 gave homesteaders another 160 acres if they planted 40 acres of trees.</li></ul>	<ul><li>The 'sodbuster' plough was invented in 1868. It broke through tangled roots easily.</li><li>Turkey Red Wheat was brought from Russia. It needed less water than other varieties, and thrived on the arid Plains.</li></ul>	<ul><li>The development of railroads did much to relieve the isolation of the homesteaders.</li></ul>

The 1862 Pacific Railroad Act

- The east coast states were crisscrossed with railroads. Politicians wanted a transcontinental railroad that would stretch across the country.

- The distances and costs were so big that no one company was able to build it, and the US government had to offer enormous sums of money to encourage companies to get involved.

- Two companies eventually agreed to build the railroad: the Union Pacific Railroad Company and the Central Pacific Railroad Company. They were lent $16 000 for every mile of track laid. In the mountains, they received $48 000 for every mile. They also received millions of acres of land to sell to future settlers.

- The two companies' tracks met at Promontory Summit, Utah in 1869 and the First Transcontinental Railroad was complete.

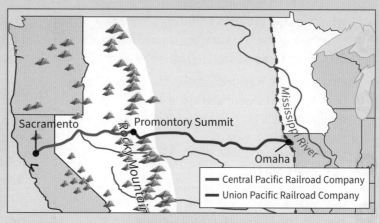

▲ The First Transcontinental Railroad ran 3077 km from Omaha in the east to Sacramento in the west

The effects of the railroad

- The railroad made the west more accessible and safer for settlers. Troops could move around more quickly and law officers could more easily reach isolated settlements.

- Living on the Plains became less isolated as the nearest town could be reached more quickly.

- The railroad made it easier to buy and sell goods. For example, goods from the east and the Plains could now be taken to ports in California to be sold in markets in Asia.

- The railroad companies used extremely effective marketing methods to sell the plots of land they had been given. They sent agents to Europe to persuade people to 'go west' and start a new life. By 1880, the railroad companies had settled over 200 million acres in the west and many towns had grown around the stations and railheads.

Continued lawlessness in the west

- Lawlessness continued to be a problem, despite the federal government increasing the number of marshals, and the local communities increasing the number of sheriffs. This was because as the population of the west continued to grow, so did the problem of criminal behaviour.

- This was especially a problem in areas where the trains stopped. New towns grew around stations and other unloading points known as railheads, and robbery, fighting, drinking, gambling, and prostitution became widespread problems.

- Many banks, businesses, and even the federal government itself, paid private police forces (such as the renowned Pinkerton Detective Agency) to help tackle crime.

 Key terms Make sure you can write a definition for these key terms

American Civil War
plantation
Confederate States of America
homestead   prove up

REVISION TIP

Many things you will study in the book, such as the building of the transcontinental railroad, had several long-term consequences. As you learn about later events, ask yourself: 'Would this have happened without the railroad?' If the answer is no, then it is a consequence of the railroad.

Retrieval

Learn the answers to the questions below, then cover the answers column with a piece of paper and write as many as you can. Check and repeat.

	Questions	Answers
1	What was the difference between the way that the northern states (the Union) and the southern states wanted to settle the west?	The northern states wanted thousands of small farms; the southern states wanted enormous plantations worked by enslaved African Americans
2	Why were the northern states (the Union) free to pass Acts that would settle the west in the way they wanted?	Because the southern states seceded from (left) the Union
3	What was the purpose of the 1862 Homestead Act?	To encourage individual families to set up small farms and prevent land in the west from being bought up by rich and powerful landowners
4	List two technological advances that made farming the Plains easier for settlers.	Two from: water drills / wind pumps / barbed wire / 'sodbuster' plough
5	How did the 1873 Timber Culture Act improve life for settlers on the Plains?	Settlers could claim another 160 acres of land if they planted 40 acres of trees
6	How large was each homestead?	160 acres
7	Identify three conditions for claiming a homestead.	Three from: pay $10 to file the claim / be the head of a family or over 21 years old / not be an Indigenous person or Confederate soldier / work the land for five years and pay another $30 to 'prove up' the claim
8	How many claims could each homesteader file?	One
9	How did the US government encourage companies to build the railroads?	Provided loans for every mile of track laid; granted the companies millions of acres of land to sell to future settlers
10	What were the start and end cities of the First Transcontinental Railroad, and where did the two subsections of the railroad meet?	Omaha in the east and Sacramento in the west; the two subsections met at Promontory Summit, Utah
11	List two reasons why the building of the railroads increased migration west.	Two from: made the west more accessible and safer / reduced isolation / enabled trade / the railroad companies encouraged people to buy the land they had been granted by the government
12	Identify one key feature of the new railroad towns.	One from: they were built around where the trains stopped / they experienced high levels of drinking, gambling, prostitution, and lawlessness

Put paper here

Previous questions

Use the questions below to check your knowledge from previous chapters.

Questions		Answers
1 Define the term 'Indigenous peoples'.		The first peoples to live in a land
2 Give two reasons why the Donner Party's journey ended in disaster.		Two from: the party set off late in the year / it took an unknown shortcut / it decided to camp in the Sierra Nevada for the winter
3 Name two types of law enforcement official.		Two from: US marshal / deputy marshal / town marshal / sheriff

Put paper here

✏ Practice

Exam-style questions

1   Explain **two** consequences of the discovery of gold in California in 1848
    for early settlement in the west.   **(8)**

2   Write a narrative account analysing the key events leading up to the opening
    of the First Transcontinental Railroad in 1869.

> You **may** use the following in your answer:
> - railroads in the east and isolation of homesteaders in the west
> - the Union Pacific Railroad and Central Pacific Railroad companies
>
> You **must** also use information of your own.

EXAM TIP

Think about a narrative account as a story. It needs a beginning, a middle, and an end. The two bullet points may only provide the middle or the end. Use your knowledge to ensure that you cover the whole story.

3   Explain **two** of the following:

- The importance of the American Civil War for the way the
    west was settled.   **(8)**

EXAM TIP

The question contains three bullet points, and you must choose two to write about in the exam. Read all three bullet points carefully before circling the two you think you can answer best.

- The importance of the 1862 Homestead Act for the development
    of settlements in the west.   **(8)**

- The importance of the transcontinental railroad for encouraging
    settlement on the Plains.   **(8)**

The growth of the cattle industry

Sedalia Trail

- In the 1850s, most of the USA's cattle herds were based in the southern state of Texas. **Ranchers** in Texas realised they could make big profits if they could transport their cattle to the growing towns in the east.

- The first **cattle drive** was down the Sedalia Trail. From there, cattle were transported by train to markets in the east.

- Unfortunately, **Texas longhorn** cattle often carried a disease called 'Texas fever'. It was harmless to the longhorns but deadly to the other cattle that homesteaders kept on the Plains. As a result, in June 1853, angry mobs of homesteaders blocked the Sedalia Trail.

- **Quarantine** laws were introduced in parts of Missouri in 1855 and in Kansas in 1859 to stop the spread of Texas fever. These laws made it illegal to bring cattle from Texas into quarantine zones, making it difficult to reach the eastern markets.

Goodnight–Loving Trail

- Charles Goodnight, a Confederate soldier, returned from the Civil War to find that his herd of 180 cattle had grown to over 5000. He realised there might be a market for his cows in the west.

- In 1866, Goodnight and his business partner, Oliver Loving, set off on their first cattle drive to Fort Sumner, New Mexico. There, the government bought the cattle to feed the soldiers in the fort and Indigenous peoples on nearby reservations. Goodnight charged four times the price he would have got for the cattle in Texas and made an enormous profit.

- In 1868, the Goodnight–Loving Trail was extended north to reach Colorado's gold-mining towns. Cattle were sold for a sizeable profit, bought to feed the men building the Transcontinental Railroad.

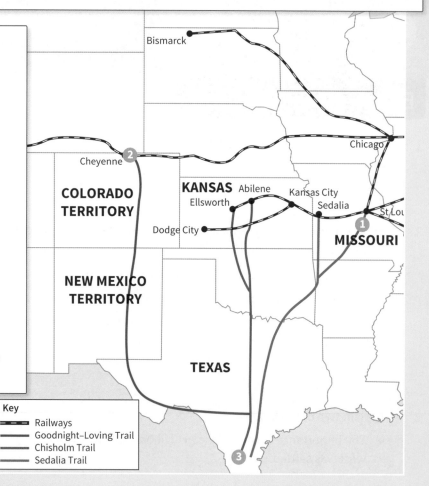

▶ *The main trails followed by the cattle drives from Texas*

Key
- ▬ Railways
- Goodnight–Loving Trail
- Chisholm Trail
- Sedalia Trail

Chisholm Trail

- A cattle dealer called Joseph McCoy realised that enormous profits could be made if ranchers drove their cows to an undeveloped area called Abilene, bypassing the quarantine zones to reach the railroad.

- In 1867, McCoy bought up land in Abilene, built stockyards to hold the cattle before they were loaded on to trains, and opened a hotel for **cowboys**. He then spent a lot of money marketing the Chisholm Trail (named after a trader called Jesse Chisholm who scouted the trail).

- The Chisholm Trail crossed Indigenous reservations and disrupted hunting. As a result, the Indigenous peoples who were affected charged 10 cents for every cow that passed through their land.

- In 1867, 36 000 cattle were driven down the Chisholm Trail to Abilene. By 1870, over 300 000 cattle made the same journey. Abilene had four hotels and ten saloons, and had become the first '**cow town**'.

The rise of the cattle barons

- The era of the cow towns such as Abilene was short-lived because of the rise of '**cattle barons**'.

- In 1861, John Iliff purchased some cattle in Colorado and discovered not only that they could survive the harsh Plains' winters but that the freezing cold killed the insects that carried Texas fever.

- He soon had 35 000 cattle on the Plains and sold animals to railroad builders, soldiers, and the Indigenous peoples. People began to copy Iliff's idea.

- The grass the cattle ate on the Plains cost nothing and the grazing lands were close to the railroad. Instead of having to be driven for thousands of kilometres, the cattle were branded with an identifying mark, left to roam free, and then rounded up once a year and taken the short distance to the railroad.

- Wealthy and powerful men started to buy enormous herds to raise on the '**open range**' of the Plains. They became known as cattle barons.

The changing role of cowboys

The move from long drives to raising cattle on the Plains greatly changed the lives of cowboys.

The life of cowboys driving on trails	The life of cowboys ranching on open range
Spent nearly all day in the saddle driving cattle for hundreds of kilometres, at an average of 24 km a day.	On the ranch with cattle; branded cattle and rounded them up.
Looked out for the welfare of the cattle and identified sick or injured animals.	Mended boundary fences and identified sick and injured animals.
Long drives only took place in the summer, so they had to earn enough money to last all year or find alternative employment in winter.	Work was all year round, but fewer cowboys were needed on ranches than on drives.
Enjoyed great freedom but faced great dangers: extreme weather, sleeping in the open, Indigenous peoples who became hostile when the drives crossed their land, stampeding cattle, crossing rivers, and quicksand.	Much safer and more comfortable occupation (they slept in bunkhouses); some conflict with Indigenous peoples, when ranches were built on reservations, and with homesteaders, particularly over water.
Often drank and gambled heavily once they reached the cow town at the end of the trail; some died in drunken gunfights.	Drinking and gambling were often banned, as were guns.

Cattle barons' conflict with homesteaders

- Cattle barons fed their enormous herd on public land for free.

- Due to the 1862 Homestead Act, more and more public land became private. Homesteaders fenced off **pasture** and water sources on their land. This angered cattle barons, who often had the barbed wire fences cut.

- Cattle barons were also angered by homesteaders feeding sheep on public pasture that they wanted for their cattle.

Key terms Make sure you can write a definition for these key terms

rancher   cattle drive   Texas longhorn   Texas fever   quarantine
cowboy   cow town   cattle baron   open range   pasture

Retrieval

Learn the answers to the questions below, then cover the answers column with a piece of paper and write as many as you can. Check and repeat.

Questions

	Questions	Answers
1	How did the American Civil War affect the development of the cattle industry?	The herds bred and increased enormously while the Texas ranchers were away fighting for the Confederate army
2	Why did cowboys drive cattle hundreds of kilometres along trails from the Texas ranches to the markets in the east?	The price of beef in the east was much higher than in Texas
3	What was Texas fever, and why was it a problem?	A disease carried by Texas longhorn cattle that infected and killed the cattle kept by homesteaders on the Plains
4	What prevented ranchers from driving their herds down the Sedalia Trail to markets in the east?	Homesteaders blocked the trail and state governments enforced quarantine zones to prevent diseased cattle from entering
5	How did Charles Goodnight and Oliver Loving make their money from cattle?	They drove their cattle west to sell to army forts, Indigenous peoples on reservations, gold miners and railroad companies
6	What was the name of the first 'cow town'?	Abilene
7	Who established the first cow town and when?	Joseph McCoy in 1867
8	What trail led to the first cow town?	Chisholm Trail
9	Who pioneered the 'open range' method of farming?	John Iliff
10	What were the advantages for cattle barons of the 'open range method of farming?	Cattle could pasture for free on public land; they didn't have to be driven long distances
11	Identify one advantage for cowboys of the open range method of farming.	One from: provided employment all year round / much safer / more comfortable (cowboys slept in bunkhouses rather than in the open)
12	How did the move to the 'open range' method of farming lead to a safer life for cowboys?	No more danger from stampedes, crossing rivers or quicksand; drinking, gambling, and guns were banned (which reduced deaths from gunfights)
13	Why did cattle barons and homesteaders come into conflict?	Cattle barons wanted the Plains, including the grass and water, to remain public property; homesteaders fenced their land and water off to keep the cattle barons' cows out; homesteaders fed their sheep on public land

Put paper here

5

Previous questions

Use the questions below to check your knowledge from previous chapters.

Questions | Answers

Questions	Answers
1 Define the term 'pioneer'.	US citizens, either from Europe or descended from Europeans, who travelled west on trails across the Plains in the 1840s and 1850s
2 Give two reasons why the Donner Party's journey ended in disaster.	Two from: the party set off late in the year / it took an unknown shortcut / it decided to camp in the Sierra Nevada for the winter
3 Give two reasons why the Fort Laramie Treaty of 1851 was significant.	Two from: it meant the end of the Permanent Indian Frontier / many Indigenous peoples were made to move to live on reservations / it increased the confidence of non-Indigenous migrants and settlers about travelling across the Plains / it aimed to resolve conflict between Indigenous nations of the Plains and non-Indigenous people crossing through the lands under their control

Put paper here

✎ Practice

Exam-style questions

1   Explain **two** consequences of Texas longhorn cattle spreading 'Texas fever' to other livestock in 1853. **(8)**

2   Write a narrative account analysing the key events in the development of tension between Indigenous Americans and migrants in the 1840s and 1850s.

> You **may** use the following in your answer:
> - Gold Rush (1849)
> - Fort Laramie Treaty (1851)
>
> You **must** also use information of your own.

3   Explain **two** of the following:
- The importance of the First Transcontinental Railroad for the development of the cattle industry. **(8)**
- The importance of the development of the open range for changing the cattle industry. **(8)**
- The importance of the 1862 Homestead Act for creating conflict between cattle ranchers and homesteaders on the Plains. **(8)**

EXAM TIP 🎯

It's always a good idea to plan your answer when writing a narrative account. It helps to give you a structure to work to. For example:

- Beginning: growing number of settlers move onto and through the Plains, increasing tension; ways of life of Indigenous peoples disrupted
- Middle: Gold rush of 1949 increased the number of migrants dramatically, increasing tension
- End: Fort Laramie Treaty (1851) attempted to reduce conflict but little was done to stop settlers who broke treaty terms, making tension a key feature of the relationship.

Knowledge

6 Changes in the ways of life of Indigenous peoples of the Plains

The impact of the railroads

The building of the railroads on the Plains disrupted Indigenous people's ability to hunt bison.

- The railroad tracks, which were often fenced off, obstructed bison migrations, meaning herds could not always cross into reservations where they could be hunted by Indigenous peoples.

- Bison were killed and used as a source of meat to feed railroad builders.

- Settlers on the Plains started to hunt bison. 'Hunting trains' enabled tourists to shoot bison in large numbers from the safety of carriages.

The impact of gold rushes

The discovery of gold led to a huge increase in the number of migrants crossing the Plains, which caused many difficulties for Indigenous peoples living there.

- The discovery of gold in the Rocky Mountains in 1859 brought about 100 000 migrants to the Colorado. They trespassed across reservations, built camps, and started to mine. Some Indigenous people were attacked and pushed from gold fields on their reservations by **prospectors**. In response, some Indigenous people attacked gold miners.

- Some Cheyenne and Arapaho chiefs appealed for a peaceful resolution. In 1861, the Fort Wise Treaty was signed between the US government and six Cheyenne and four Arapaho tribes, but the majority of Cheyenne opposed the treaty because they did not agree with its terms, did not think the US government had the right to tell them what to do, and did not trust that the government would keep its word anyway.

- When large deposits of gold were discovered in Montana in 1863, it attracted fortune hunters from the east and those who had been unsuccessful in Colorado. Many took a shortcut to the gold fields, called the Bozeman Trail, that cut right through land that had been promised to the Lakota in the Fort Laramie Treaty of 1851.

The impact of the cattle industry

The growth of the cattle industry created conflict between cattle farmers and Indigenous peoples, and further reduced the herds of bison that Indigenous peoples depended on.

- The cattle drives north from Texas often crossed land that had been formally allocated to the governments of Indigenous nations by treaty. Some Indigenous nations charged a fee, and the cattle drives were allowed to continue. Other nations, such as the Comanche, attacked cowboys, which led the US army to retaliate.

- Cattle ate the same food as bison – the grass on the Plains. The development of open range farming meant that the number of cattle on the Plains increased from 130 000 in 1860 to 4.5 million in 1880. Without adequate food, the number of bison declined.

Indigenous people's resistance

Indigenous nations of the Plains faced huge challenges at this time as US treaty promises were broken and instead nations faced food shortages and incursions by non-Indigenous settlers. Despite the risks, violent resistance increased into a series of conflicts known in the US as the 'Indian Wars', which included these events:

Little Crow's War (1862)	The Sand Creek Massacre (1864)	Red Cloud's War (1866–68)

Little Crow's War (1862)

Background	Main events	Conclusion
• Around 12 000 people of the Santee nation moved to a reservation near Minnesota. They tried to adapt to a life of farming but, when crops failed, they relied on government payments to survive. • In 1862, the American Civil War delayed the government payment. The government agency store on the reservation refused to sell food on credit. • The Santee faced starvation.	• In August 1862, four young Santee men, returning from an unsuccessful hunt, attacked and killed five settlers. • The Santee leader, Little Crow, led an attack on the government agency store, killing 20 men and capturing ten women and children. • A troop of 45 soldiers sent to the reservation was ambushed and 21 soldiers were killed. • Little Crow continued to lead raids on army forts and settlers' towns, yet he was unable to rally other Indigenous nations to his cause. • Around 700 settlers were killed in numerous attacks. Huge numbers of army reinforcements were sent to quash the Santee.	• By September 1862, it was clear that the Santee could not continue their resistance without huge losses. Little Crow headed west with some of his followers. • By October 1862, over 2000 of those who remained on the reservation had surrendered or been captured. • A military court sentenced 303 Santee men to death. President Abraham Lincoln reduced the sentences of all but 38. These 38 men were publicly hanged in December 1862. • During the first winter after they were relocated to a reservation with poor soil and contaminated water, 400 Santee died.

The Sand Creek Massacre (1864)

Background	Main events	Conclusion
• The Cheyenne faced starvation because there were so few bison and because the Sand Creek reservation was unsuitable for growing crops. • Groups of Cheyenne started raiding settlers' wagon trains and mining camps for food and resources.	• In 1864, after three years of raids, the Cheyenne chief, Black Kettle, tried to bring peace by negotiating with the US government. • The talks were unsuccessful, but Black Kettle believed he had secured government protection for his people. • He led 700 Cheyenne to camp at Sand Creek. • At daybreak on 29 November 1864, Colonel Chivington and 1000 Colorado volunteers surrounded Black Kettle's camp. • The Cheyenne had no military defences against this surprise attack. Black Kettle escaped, but 163 people – including many women and children – were massacred and their bodies mutilated.	• News of the massacre quickly spread. A government committee declared Chivington had 'deliberately planned and executed a foul and dastardly massacre'. • The Cheyenne, Arapaho, and Lakota were united in their horror and retaliated with widespread attacks on ranches and settlements, with many settler families killed. • Eventually, in late 1865, a Government Peace Commission compelled the Indigenous nations to end the war and move to new reservations.

⚙ Knowledge

6 Changes in the ways of life of Indigenous peoples of the Plains

Red Cloud's War (1866–68)

Background	Main events	Conclusion
• Gold prospectors using the Bozeman Trail to access the gold fields of Montana trespassed on Lakota lands, breaking the terms of the 1851 Fort Laramie Treaty. • The government did nothing to stop this from happening. • Some Lakota bands started to attack the trespassers.	• In 1866, the US government started peace talks with the Lakota leader, Red Cloud. However, at the same time, they ordered the construction of several forts along the Bozeman Trail on Lakota land. • When Red Cloud learned of this, he immediately broke off the talks and began to attack the army. Although the Lakota and their allies were not able to capture the forts, they did manage to trick a detachment of 80 men into leaving Fort Phil Kearny. All 80 men, under the command of Captain William Fetterman, were killed in an incident known as 'Fetterman's Trap'. • By surrounding the forts, Red Cloud ensured that no soldier could safely leave, and no settler could use the Bozeman Trail. • Red Cloud managed to unite Lakota, Arapaho, and Cheyenne to fight with him throughout the winter months.	• Red Cloud's War forced the US government and army to admit defeat. They had to negotiate a second Fort Laramie Treaty in 1868, in which they agreed to abandon the forts on the Bozeman Trail. When the soldiers left, the Lakota burned the forts to the ground. • The Treaty also created a new reservation, called the Great Sioux Reservation. • Red Cloud promised never to lead his men in attacks on settlers again.

▲ A US depiction of US soldiers being attacked by Red Cloud's warriors on the Bozeman Trail in 1866. All 80 of the soldiers were killed in what became known as 'Fetterman's Trap'

US government policy towards Indigenous peoples

- By the late 1860s it was clear that the existing government policy towards Indigenous peoples was being resisted. Settlers were not being stopped from breaking the Fort Laramie Treaty of 1851 and some Indigenous peoples rejected the Treaty terms or lost any trust in the US government. The result was escalating conflict and bloodshed on the Plains.

- Some people, such as the US army's General Sherman, believed the only solution to resistance was to exterminate (kill) Indigenous peoples.

- However, when Ulysses S. Grant became President of the USA in 1869, he took a different approach to resolving conflict with Indigenous peoples, which he called the Indian Peace Policy.

Problem	President Grant's solution
Small reservations meant it was impossible for Indigenous peoples to survive by hunting. They therefore became reliant on US government handouts and lost their independence.	Invest $2 million to fund an education programme to teach Indigenous peoples how to farm crops, read and write, and do simple maths. Indigenous peoples would then be able to **assimilate** and succeed in US society.
The agents who worked for the US government's Bureau of Indian Affairs were often corrupt. They used their position to cheat Indigenous peoples out of money and goods they received from the government.	Appoint agents with a strong Christian faith. Devout Christians were considered less likely to cheat Indigenous peoples. They would also work to convert Indigenous people to Christianity. Ely Parker, an Indigenous American (birth name: Hasanoanda), was appointed Commissioner of Indian Affairs.
Settlers and gold prospectors travelled through, farmed, and mined land that had been promised to Indigenous peoples.	Instruct the army to protect reservations from trespassers.

The impact of Grant's peace policy

The effect of Grant's peace policy was limited.

- Many Indigenous Americans resisted the idea of assimilation, which they saw as an attempt to destroy Indigenous cultures. To them, 'living like US citizens' meant accepting a totally different view of the land and the world. Many Indigenous Americans could not accept this. In an interview in 1894, Big Eagle, a Lakota chief, said:

> The whites were always trying to make the Indians give up their life and live like white men, go to farming, work hard and do as they did, and the Indians did not know how to do that, and did not want to anyway.

- Any Indigenous peoples who did not stay on their reservation after Grant's peace policy was introduced were classified as 'hostile' and left open to attack from the US army.

- Ely Parker was forced to resign from his position as Commissioner of Indian Affairs in 1871, after what many believed was a racially motivated campaign against him.

- Food distributed to Indigenous peoples through the government agency stores continued to be of very poor quality.

- Grant's peace policy ultimately failed to bring peace to the Plains and there was further conflict at the Battle of the Little Big Horn in 1876.

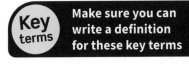

Make sure you can write a definition for these key terms

prospector   assimilate

Learn the answers to the questions below, then cover the answers column with a piece of paper and write as many as you can. Check and repeat.

Questions | Answers

1 Identify two ways in which the arrival of the railroads impacted the lives of Indigenous peoples on the Plains.

Two from: the tracks obstructed bison migrations / 'hunting trains' enabled tourists to kill bison in large numbers / bison were killed for meat to feed railroad builders / many more people settled on the Plains

2 How were the lives of Indigenous peoples disrupted by the discovery of gold in the Rocky Mountains in 1859?

Gold miners trespassed across Indigenous reservations, built camps, and started to mine

3 Where were large deposits of gold discovered in 1863?

Montana

4 What was the Bozeman Trail and why was it a problem?

A shortcut to the Montana gold fields that cut through land allocated to the Lakota in the Fort Laramie Treaty of 1851

5 How did developments in the cattle industry lead to a reduction in the number of bison?

Open range farming meant that by 1880, 4.5 million cattle were on the Plains, which reduced the amount of grass available for the bison to feed on

6 Which events led to Little Crow's War?

The Santee were facing starvation and unable to buy food on credit from US government stores; Santee young men attacked and killed settlers and soldiers

7 Who led the regiment of 1000 volunteers responsible for the Sand Creek Massacre?

Colonel Chivington

8 Who was the Cheyenne chief who escaped the Sand Creek Massacre?

Black Kettle

9 When and how did Red Cloud's War end?

The war ended in 1868 with the US government and army defeated; they left the Bozeman Trail and signed a second Fort Laramie Treaty, which created a new Great Sioux Reservation

10 Identify two problems with the policies towards Indigenous peoples before 1869.

Two from: reservations were too small to support survival by hunting bison / agents who distributed government supplies were corrupt / trespassers entered Indigenous lands without punishment

11 Which US President introduced the Indian Peace Policy?

Ulysses S. Grant

12 Name two of the main features of the Indian Peace Policy.

Two from: funding an education programme to enable Indigenous peoples to assimilate in US society / appointing agents with a strong Christian faith / instructing the army to protect reservations from trespassers

Put paper here

Previous questions

Use the questions below to check your knowledge from previous chapters.

Questions		Answers
1 List two things that 'pulled' settlers west.		Two from: the promise of fertile farmland, freedom and adventure / discovery of the Oregon Trail / 1841 Pre-emption Act allowed settlers to buy land cheaply / gold discovered in California in 1848
2 How large was each homestead?		160 acres
3 What trail led to the first cow town?		Chisholm Trail

Put paper here   Put paper here

✏ Practice

Exam-style questions

1   Explain **two** consequences of Ulysses S. Grant's Indian Peace Policy of 1869.

(8)

> **EXAM TIP**
> When answering this question, make sure you describe the key events in chronological order. Aim to include the year or years in which each event took place.

2   Write a narrative account analysing the key events in the development of the cattle industry in the 1860s.

(8)

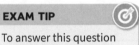

> You **may** use the following in your answer:
> - Goodnight–Loving Trail
> - Abilene
>
> You **must** also use information of your own.

3   Explain **two** of the following:

- The importance of the cattle industry for creating conflict between Indigenous peoples and the US government.

(8)

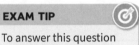

- The importance of gold prospecting for creating conflict between Indigenous peoples and the US government.

(8)

- The importance of reservations for causing the 'Indian Wars' of the 1860s.

(8)

> **EXAM TIP**
> To answer this question successfully, remember to link the focus of the question (e.g., conflict between Indigenous people and the US government) to the event, person or development covered by the bullet point (e.g., the cattle industry). Don't spend a long time describing the conflict between Indigenous people and the US government, and the cattle industry. Spend your time explaining the significance of the cattle industry for the conflict.

⚙ Knowledge

7 Changes in farming, the cattle industry, and settlement, 1876–95

The impact of new technology and new farming methods

Farmers in the American West continued to face many challenges. However, the invention of new technologies and farming methods had a positive impact.

Wind pumps became more powerful and reliable. They could now draw water from hundreds of metres underground.

New technologies and farming methods after 1876

Improvements to the 'sodbuster' plough made farming dry ground easier. The plough also became more affordable, as did other machinery, such as binders, threshers, and reapers. The railroads made equipment more widely available to farmers, too.

The new technique of '**dry farming**' preserved moisture in the soil by preventing evaporation. This meant wheat could be grown very successfully on the arid Plains.

Changes in the cattle industry

With enormous profits to be made, the cattle barons' herds grew larger and larger.

↓

This increased demand on the grass of the Plains, especially during droughts. The lack of pasture led to many cattle becoming weak.

↓

The supply of beef was soon greater than the demand for it.

↓

The price of beef dropped.

↓

Lower prices meant lower profits for the cattle barons. Some went **bankrupt**. Others held on to their cattle in the hope that prices would rise again.

↓

Large numbers of underfed cattle went into the harsh winter of 1886–87. Deep snow prevented them from reaching grass or water and an estimated 30 per cent of cattle on the Plains died.

↓

More cattle barons went bankrupt. Others began to change how they raised cattle.

The winter of 1886–87 also led to changes in the lives of cowboys.

- Many cowboys died searching for cattle in the deep snow.
- Smaller ranches required fewer cowboys, so many lost their jobs.
- Those who kept their jobs continued to brand cattle and repair ranch buildings. They also harvested the hay used to feed the herd over winter.

For many farmers, the punishing winter of 1886–87 meant the end of the open range.

- The ranchers that were still in business after that winter shifted to raising smaller herds that could be sheltered indoors in extreme weather.
- They fenced in their herds using barbed wire, meaning the cattle were easier to monitor and protect from thieves (cattle rustlers).
- Fenced-in pastures also meant different breeds of cattle could be kept separate from each other, so higher quality meat could be produced.

Key terms Make sure you can write a definition for these key terms

dry farming   bankrupt   Exodusters   land rush   census

Continued settlement on the Plains

US citizens continued to move to the Plains as people attempted to start new lives and the government allocated more land to settlers.

The Exoduster movement

After the American Civil War, slavery was banned in the southern states. In 1879, around 43 000 formerly enslaved African Americans left the south and headed west. The majority settled in Kansas, but many settled in other western states and territories, including Oklahoma, Colorado, and Arizona. These settlers became known as the **Exodusters**.

The Exodusters' name was inspired by a Bible story. The book of Exodus describes how God rescued a whole nation from enslavement, with people walking long distances to freedom. This inspired many African Americans in the southern states to migrate to Kansas.

Why did the Exodusters move west?

Many previously enslaved African Americans continued to experience appalling oppression and violence from former slaveholders in the southern states.

The 1862 Homestead Act enabled those who had previously been enslaved to claim 160 acres of land in the west.

Many African Americans were inspired by a false rumour that the US government had given the whole state of Kansas to people who had once been enslaved.

A formerly enslaved African American, Benjamin Singleton, a community leader and businessman, helped many African Americans living in the south to make the long journey to Kansas.

- Most Exodusters were very poor and didn't have money to invest in a farm. They also found that the best land in Kansas had already been taken.

- Many white residents did not welcome the Exodusters or support the Governor of Kansas when he gave money to the new arrivals to help them settle and survive.

- By 1880, word had spread that Kansas had not, in fact, been granted to African Americans and mass migration stopped.

- The Exodusters who settled in Kansas enjoyed fewer rights and were usually poorer than settlers who weren't formerly enslaved.

The Oklahoma land rushes

- In 1889, the US government opened up 2 million acres of land in Oklahoma to settlers. The land had been designated as Indigenous land but hadn't been allocated to a specific nation or tribe.

- At noon on 22 April 1889, a cannon was fired to signal the start of the first Oklahoma **land rush**, and thousands of people raced to reach plot markers and claim their 160 acres.

- More land rushes took place in Oklahoma. The biggest was in 1893, when 6 million acres of the

'Cherokee strip' was given to settlers by the US government, despite protests from the Cherokee nation. The land had been promised to the Cherokee 60 years earlier.

- The 1890 **census** revealed that, unlike in 1880, there was no 'barrier' between the United States and Indigenous lands. US citizens had settled everywhere from east to west. The US Census Bureau declared the 'Indian Frontier' closed.

Retrieval

Learn the answers to the questions below, then cover the answers column with a piece of paper and write as many as you can. Check and repeat.

Questions	Answers
1 How did technology further improve settlers' ability to farm on the Plains after 1876?	Improved wind pumps and ploughs; access to affordable new machinery such as binders, threshers, and reapers
2 How did the 'dry farming' technique help farmers grow crops on the Plains?	It prevented water in the soil from evaporating
3 What led to a drop in the price of beef?	The herds grew too big, and supply became greater than demand
4 Why did so many cattle die in the winter of 1886–87?	The herds were already underfed; heavy snowfall meant they couldn't reach grass to eat or water to drink
5 How did the winter of 1886–87 change cattle ranching on the Plains?	Cattle were no longer raised on the open range but were kept in smaller herds on pasture fenced off with barbed wire
6 Who were the Exodusters?	Previously enslaved African Americans who migrated from the southern states in 1879 in search of a better quality of life
7 Where did the Exodusters move to?	Western states and territories such as Kansas, Oklahoma, and Colorado
8 Name two things that inspired the Exodusters to migrate.	Two from: oppression and violence from former slaveholders / Bible book of Exodus / rumour that Kansas had been granted to formerly enslaved African Americans; work of Benjamin Singleton / right to claim 160 acres of land in the west thanks to the 1862 Homestead Act
9 Give two reasons why many Exodusters struggled after migrating.	Two from: they were poor so unable to invest in farming / they received limited help from the state government / they had fewer rights than other settlers
10 What was a 'land rush'?	When people rushed to claim plots of land allocated for settlement by the government
11 Why did land rushes take place in Oklahoma in 1889 and 1893?	The US government opened up millions of acres of land for settlement
12 Why did the US Census Bureau declare the 'Indian Frontier' closed in 1890?	The 1890 census recorded that US citizens occupied land in every area from east to west, meaning there was no longer a barrier between the USA and Indigenous lands

Put paper here

Previous questions

Use the questions below to check your knowledge from previous chapters.

Questions	Answers
1 Identify one key feature of the new railroad towns.	One from: they were built around where the trains stopped / they experienced high levels of drinking, gambling, prostitution, and lawlessness
2 What was the name of the first 'cow town'?	Abilene
3 Why did cattle barons and homesteaders come into conflict?	Cattle barons wanted the Plains, including the grass and water, to remain public property; homesteaders fenced their land and water off to keep the cattle barons' cows out; homesteaders fed their sheep on public land

Put paper here

✏ Practice

Exam-style questions

1   Explain **two** consequences of the winter of 1886–87 for cattle ranching on the Plains.   **(8)**

EXAM TIP
Remember to use names, dates, and other details to fully explain each consequence.

2   Write a narrative account analysing the key events of the 'Indian Wars' of the 1860s.   **(8)**

> You **may** use the following in your answer:
> • Little Crow's War (1862)
> • the Sand Creek Massacre (1864)
> You **must** also use information of your own.

EXAM TIP
Pay close attention to the dates or period the question is asking about. You will not be rewarded if your answer discusses conflicts involving Indigenous peoples that occurred before or after the 1860s.

3   Explain **two** of the following:
   • The importance of the Homestead Act for the development of the Exoduster movement.   **(8)**

   • The importance of the development of new technology and techniques for farming on the Plains between 1876 and 1895.   **(8)**

   • The importance of barbed wire for the development of ranching on the Plains after the winter of 1886–87.   **(8)**

⚙ Knowledge

8 Lawlessness and conflict

The problem of lawlessness in the 1880s and 1890s

- Lawlessness continued to be a problem in the American West during the 1880s and 1890s despite the appointment of more marshals and sheriffs.
- Criminals and law enforcement officers became internationally famous and helped promote the idea of a 'wild west'.
- However, unlike previous lawlessness, much of the crime in the 1880s and 1890s was due to struggles over land between mining companies, homesteaders, and cattle barons.

Billy the Kid

- Billy the Kid – born William H. Bonney, Jr. – is probably the most famous criminal of the American West.
- He rose to fame during the Lincoln County War of 1878. This was a **range war** between rival cattle barons. When one of the barons, John Henry Tunstall, was murdered, a posse called the Regulators was formed to avenge his death. Among the posse's members was Billy the Kid.
- Around 19 people were killed in the Lincoln County War, including a sheriff and his deputy whom the Regulators believed had sided with the rival barons.
- A new sheriff named Pat Garrett tracked down and shot Billy the Kid dead in 1881.

The Johnson County War (1892)

- The Johnson County War was a range war in Wyoming, between a powerful group of cattle barons known as the Wyoming Stock Growers Association (WSGA) and homesteaders who kept small herds of cattle.
- The WSGA members were unhappy about the amount of public land being fenced off by homesteaders. They also suspected the homesteaders were stealing their young cattle before they were branded.
- Homesteaders Ella Watson and Jim Averill fenced off land that had previously been used by WSGA member Albert Bothwell for his cattle. When Watson obtained a small herd of cows, Bothwell accused her of rustling. He hanged both Watson and Averill and took back the land. More homesteaders were also murdered.
- The remaining homesteaders held a spring round-up of cattle, much earlier than the WSGA. The cattle barons believed the homesteaders were doing this so they could steal young, **unbranded** WSGA cattle.
- The WSGA raised $100 000 and hired 22 gunmen to 'invade' Johnson County and kill 70 homesteaders suspected of rustling. The plan failed as the sheriff of Johnson County surrounded and arrested the gunmen before they could act.
- Although law and order triumphed over vigilantism, the wealthy WSGA used its power and influence to stop the gunmen from being prosecuted.

Wyatt Earp and the gunfight at the OK Corral (1881)

- Wyatt Earp is probably the most famous law enforcement official of the American West, although many believe he was as much a criminal as a lawman.
- Despite several arrests for cattle rustling in his youth, he became a deputy marshal. He was then appointed deputy sheriff in the mining town of Tombstone, where a powerful mining company was in a power struggle with small ranchers.
- Earp and his brothers shot dead three ranchers at the OK Corral in 1886. Morgan Earp was then killed in a revenge shooting. Wyatt Earp immediately killed two men he blamed for his brother's death.
- Tombstone turned against the Earps as lawlessness continued to increase. They were accused of acting as if they were above the law by committing crimes such as robbery and murder. They left Tombstone in 1882.

Growing tensions between the US government and Indigenous peoples of the Plains

- From 1876, the US government and army continued to engage in conflict with Indigenous peoples.
- The Battle of Greasy Grass, named the Battle of Little Bighorn by US citizens at the time, in 1876 and the Wounded Knee Massacre of 1890 were the most notable of these conflicts.
- These events resulted in enormous suffering for Indigenous peoples and are often seen as the end of armed resistance to the settlement of the Plains by US citizens. The fight of Indigenous peoples for their rights continues to the present day.

The Battle of the Little Bighorn (1876)

- After Red Cloud's War in 1866–68, the Lakota had been given a reservation that contained the sacred Black Hills of Montana. Under the terms of the second Fort Laramie Treaty of 1868, no settlers were able to move onto this land.
- In 1874, Lieutenant Colonel George Custer entered Lakota land to protect nearby railroad workers, and also to look for gold in the Black Hills. When gold was discovered, news quickly spread, and a gold rush began.
- The US government offered the Lakota $6 million or $400 000 a year to mine the Black Hills. The Lakota refused and, under the leadership of Sitting Bull and Crazy Horse, around 7000 Lakota and their Cheyenne allies readied themselves for war.

- More government troops were sent for. However, the ambitious Custer wanted to defeat the Sioux alone, so he attacked their camp by Little Bighorn River.
- Custer was defeated and killed, along with all 225 of his men.

Consequences

- US public opinion demanded that the US Army destroy the Lakota as a military force.
- Two new forts were built on the Plains.
- The Lakota and Cheyenne were pursued relentlessly back to their reservations. Sitting Bull retreated to Canada, Crazy Horse surrendered in 1877.
- The Lakota were forced to give up horses and weapons, and the Black Hills were taken from them.

The Wounded Knee Massacre (1890)

- By 1890, little remained of the old way of life for Indigenous peoples on reservations. They faced starvation as their crops had failed and supplies from the government had been cut.
- Many Indigenous people began to believe that if they performed a ritual dance called the Ghost Dance, their dead ancestors would return, and all the settlers would be washed away in a great flood.
- More and more people started to dance and, fearing it might lead to rebellion, the army was called in to stop them.
- When soldiers tried to disarm a band of Lakota led by Chief Big Foot at Wounded Knee Creek, some of his band began to perform the Ghost Dance.

A gun was fired (it's not known who did this), which triggered a brutal response from the army. When the shooting stopped, 250 Lakota lay dead, including many women and children, and 25 US soldiers had been killed – most killed by their own side by mistake.

Consequences

- The Wounded Knee Massacre is often seen as the end of armed resistance by Indigenous peoples of the Plains.
- However, resistance continued in the fight for Indigenous civil rights in the 20th century and into the present day.

Key terms Make sure you can write a definition for these key terms

range war   unbranded

Retrieval

Learn the answers to the questions below, then cover the answers column with a piece of paper and write as many as you can. Check and repeat.

	Questions	Answers
1	Who were the Regulators?	A posse formed during the Lincoln County War of 1878 and including Billy the Kid
2	Who shot Billy the Kid dead, and when?	Pat Garrett, the new sheriff, in 1881
3	Name the town where Wyatt Earp was deputy sheriff.	Tombstone
4	Where and when did Earp and his brothers shoot dead three ranchers?	The OK Corral in 1881
5	Where and when did the Johnson County War take place?	Wyoming in 1892
6	What was the WSGA?	The Wyoming Stock Growers Association – a powerful group of wealthy cattle barons
7	Why were the members of the WSGA angry with homesteaders on the Plains?	Homesteaders were fencing off public land used by the WSGA to raise cattle; they were also suspected of rustling (stealing) unbranded WSGA calves
8	Which two homesteaders did Albert Bothwell hanged?	Ella Watson and Jim Averill
9	List the key events leading up to the Battle of the Little Bighorn.	Discovery of gold in the Black Hills caused a gold rush; settlers broke the 1868 Fort Laramie Treaty; the Lakota refused to allow the Black Mountains to be mined; the Lakota and their allies raised 7000 warriors ready for war; Custer attacked the Lakota camp
10	Why might some people blame Custer for the US army's defeat at the Little Bighorn?	He did not wait for reinforcements before attacking
11	Identify two consequences of the US army defeat at the Battle of the Little Bighorn.	Two from: US public opinion demanded retaliation against Indigenous peoples / two new forts were built on the Plains / the Lakota and Cheyenne were pursued back to their reservations / Sitting Bull and Crazy Horse retreated and surrendered / the Lakota were forced to give up their horses and weapons, and the Black Hills were taken from them – despite the terms of the 1868 Fort Laramie Treaty
12	Why did many Indigenous Americans perform the Ghost Dance in 1890?	They believed it would cause their dead ancestors to return and all the settlers to be washed away in a great flood
13	How did the Wounded Knee Massacre impact Indigenous peoples of the Plains?	It resulted in the killing of 250 Indigenous people; it was the Indigenous peoples' last armed resistance against US expansion; it gave the USA confidence that it was in full control of the west

Put paper here

Previous questions

Use the questions below to check your knowledge from previous chapters.

Questions		Answers
1 How did the 1873 Timber Culture Act improve life for settlers on the Plains?	Put paper here	Settlers could claim another 160 acres of land if they planted 40 acres of trees
2 How did Charles Goodnight and Oliver Loving make their money from cattle?		They drove their cattle west to sell to army forts, Indigenous people on reservations, gold miners and railroad companies
3 Identify two problems with the policies towards Indigenous peoples before 1869.	Put paper here	Two from: reservations were too small to support survival by hunting / agents who distributed government supplies were corrupt / trespassers entered Indigenous lands without punishment

✏ Practice

Exam-style questions

1 Explain **two** consequences of gold being discovered in the Black Hills of Montana in 1874. **(8)**

2 Write a narrative account analysing the key events of the Johnson County War of 1892. **(8)**

> You **may** use the following in your answer:
> - the deaths of Ella Watson and James Averill
> - the WSGA hiring 22 gunmen
>
> You **must** also use information of your own.

3 Explain **two** of the following:
- The importance of push factors in the 1840s and 1850s for encouraging westward migration. **(8)**

- The importance of the Oregon and California trails for encouraging westward migration in the 1840s and 1850s. **(8)**

- The importance of Brigham Young for the successful establishment of a Morman settlement at the Great Salt Lake. **(8)**

EXAM TIP ⊙

Consequences are things that happen because of an event, so make sure you answer Question 1 using causation language, such as 'Consequently…', 'Therefore…', 'As a result…', 'Due to this…', and 'Subsequently…'.

EXAM TIP ⊙

Remember that the two bullet points are there to help you into the narrative account. Make sure you use at least three events in your answer though, and write about them in the order in which they happened.

Knowledge

9 Indigenous peoples of the Plains: further changes to their ways of life

The extermination of the bison

In 1840, around 13 million bison lived on the Plains. By 1885, there were just 200. This extermination of the bison was central to the destruction of Indigenous peoples' traditional ways of life.

 Railroad companies killed large numbers of bison to feed the workers laying tracks.

Homesteaders and ranchers fenced off land, which stopped the bison reaching the grass they fed on.

How were the bison herds destroyed?

 From 1871, new techniques meant bison hides could be turned into leather. Both the demand for bison leather goods and the price of bison hides increased. Hunters flooded onto the Plains. William 'Buffalo Bill' Cody claimed he killed 4280 bison in a 17-month period.

Hunters could also make money from selling the skeletons of bison. They were transported east to make products such as fertiliser, glue, knife handles, and buttons.

- Without herds of bison to sustain them, Indigenous peoples could not easily leave the reservations and return to their old ways of life.
- Although it was never the official policy of the US government to destroy the bison herds, many people suspect they deliberately allowed it to happen. Certainly, neither the US government nor the US army did anything to stop the slaughter.

Changing attitudes towards the reservations

From the mid-1870s, it was clear to both Indigenous peoples and the US government that there were major issues with the reservation system.

Indigenous peoples wanted an end to the reservations because...	The US government wanted an end to the reservations because...
<ul><li>They had become unable to feed or clothe themselves without US government aid.</li><li>It was hard to maintain Indigenous culture and independence, especially when children were taken away to be educated in the USA.</li><li>Diseases introduced by settlers, such as influenza, measles, and whooping cough, were widespread on reservations.</li><li>The reservations were often situated far away from their ancestral lands and sacred places.</li></ul>	<ul><li>They knew that voters thought Indigenous Americans were getting too many handouts and were an expensive burden.</li><li>They wanted Indigenous peoples to assimilate into US society and become Christians and farmers.</li><li>They wanted to reduce the influence of chiefs and break the structures of Indigenous society.</li></ul>

Changes in US government policy towards Indigenous peoples

After 1870, the US government changed its policy towards Indigenous peoples. It now sought to break up tribal lands and assimilate the Indigenous peoples into US society.

The 1871 Indian Appropriations Act

- This Act stated that the US government would no longer treat Indigenous nations as separate and **sovereign nations** (as the USA treated Mexico or France, for example).

- From 1871, Indigenous peoples of America were legally defined as '**wards** of the US government'. This meant the government was responsible for their protection, in much the same way as a parent is responsible for their child.

The 1887 Dawes General Allotment Act

- Also referred to as the Dawes Act, this law broke up the reservations into individual family plots of 160 acres. Individuals without families were given 80 acres.

- By accepting a plot of land, Indigenous peoples accepted they were **citizens** of the United States. This meant leaving behind their nations, traditions, and ways of life to assimilate with new settlers.

- Indigenous people were forbidden from selling their allotments for 25 years.

- Reservation land that had not been allotted was sold to non-Indigenous settlers by the government.

The consequences for Indigenous peoples

- The Dawes Act broke up Indigenous communities by encouraging Indigenous peoples to act as individuals. This meant they no longer needed to consult their chiefs or councils.

- As a result of the Dawes Act, land that had belonged to entire nations was now the property of private individuals.

- Many Indigenous peoples struggled to make a success of farming, because the land they had been given was often of poor quality, and they were inexperienced in ranching and agriculture. Many sold their allotment of land as soon as they could, and many were tricked into selling it for a very low price.

- By 1890, Indigenous peoples owned half the land they had in 1887. The Dawes Act enabled the US government to reclaim 90 million acres of land from Indigenous tribes, the majority of which was sold on to non-Indigenous US citizens.

- The 1890 **census** removed all reference to a 'frontier' between the United States and the 'wilderness' that belonged to Indigenous peoples. The USA now felt it had complete control of the west.

Key terms

Make sure you can write a definition for these key terms

sovereign nation   ward   citizen   census

Retrieval

Learn the answers to the questions below, then cover the answers column with a piece of paper and write as many as you can. Check and repeat.

Questions

Answers

1 How many bison were living on the Plains in 1840 and how many in 1885?

Around 13 million in 1840 and 200 in 1885

2 Give two reasons why bison were increasingly hunted by the 1870s.

Two from: railroad companies used bison as food for workers / new production processes meant bison hides could be turned into leather / bison bones were used to make products such as fertiliser, glue, knife handles, and buttons

3 How did homesteads and ranches contribute to the decline in the number of bison living on the Plains?

They fenced off areas where bison usually fed on grass, reducing their supply of food

4 Why might the US government have deliberately allowed the bison herds to be exterminated?

Without herds of bison, Indigenous peoples could not leave their reservations to return to their old ways of life

5 Give two reasons why the reservation system had failed by the 1870s

Two from: few Indigenous people had moved to making a successful living from farming / most Indigenous people had to rely on government rations to survive / government annuities and rations were not delivered or were stolen by corrupt US officials / the reservations did not prevent conflict on the Plains / the reservations failed to help Indigenous people retain their identity and independence

6 Why did the US government want to bring an end to the reservation system by the mid-1870s?

The reservations were seen by voters as an expensive burden; the government wanted Indigenous people to assimilate into US society (by becoming Christian farmers); the government wanted to reduce the influence of chiefs and break up the structures of Indigenous societies

7 How was the 1871 Indian Appropriations Act significant for Indigenous peoples of America?

The US government would no longer treat Indigenous peoples of America as separate, sovereign nations but as wards of the USA

8 How did the 1887 Dawes General Allotment Act change the reservations?

The reservations were split into family plots of 160 acres; individuals without families were given 80 acres

9 How did the Dawes Act help to break up Indigenous communities?

Breaking up the reservations into plots meant that Indigenous peoples would now act as individuals and no longer consult their chiefs or councils

10 How was the 1890 census significant for Indigenous peoples of America?

The census removed all reference to a frontier between the United States and Indigenous lands

Put paper here

Previous questions

Use the questions below to check your knowledge from previous chapters.

Questions	Answers
1 What were the start and end cities of the First Transcontinental Railroad, and where did the two subsections of the railroad meet?	Omaha in the east and Sacramento in the west; the two subsections met at Promontory Summit, Utah
2 What prevented ranchers from driving their herds down the Sedalia Trail to markets in the east?	Homesteaders blocked the trail and state governments enforced quarantine zones to prevent diseased cattle from entering
3 Who led the regiment of 1000 volunteers responsible for the Sand Creek Massacre?	Colonel Chivington

Put paper here

Practice

Exam-style questions

1 Explain **two** consequences of the Dawes General Allotment Act of 1887. **(8)**

EXAM TIP

Make sure you explain only two consequences; you will not gain more marks for explaining more. Choose the two you feel most confident about.

2 Write a narrative account analysing the key events of the Exoduster movement of 1879. **(8)**

You **may** use the following in your answer:
- the outlawing of slavery in the southern states
- the reaction of the existing settlers in Kansas to the Exodusters' arrival

You **must** also use information of your own.

EXAM TIP

You have just over 50 minutes to answer three questions on the American West. This means you should spend around:
- 10 minutes on question 1
- 10 minutes on question 2
- 20 minutes on question 3.

This will also allow you time to plan and check your answers.

3 Explain **two** of the following:
- The importance of the railroads for the extermination of the bison herds. **(8)**
- The importance of the extermination of the bison herds for the destruction of Indigenous peoples' traditional ways of life. **(8)**
- The importance of the Dawes General Allotment Act of 1887 for destroying Indigenous peoples' ways of life. **(8)**

Great Clarendon Street, Oxford, OX2 6DP, United Kingdom

Oxford University Press is a department of the University of Oxford. It furthers the University's objective of excellence in research, scholarship, and education by publishing worldwide. Oxford is a registered trade mark of Oxford University Press in the UK and in certain other countries.

Written by James Ball

Series Editor: Aaron Wilkes

The moral rights of the author have been asserted

First published in 2023

British Library Cataloguing in Publication Data
Data available

978-1-38-204039-6

10 9 8 7 6 5 4 3 2 1

The manufacturing process conforms to the environmental regulations of the country of origin.

Printed in the UK by Bell and Bain Ltd, Glasgow

Acknowledgements
The publisher and authors would like to thank the following for permission to use photographs and other copyright material:

Photos: p12: Phil Cardamone / Alamy Stock Photo; **p28:** GRANGER - Historical Picture Archive / Alamy Stock Photo.

Artwork by Newgen.

Although we have made every effort to trace and contact all copyright holders before publication this has not been possible in all cases. If notified, the publisher will rectify any errors or omissions at the earliest opportunity.

Links to third party websites are provided by Oxford in good faith and for information only. Oxford disclaims any responsibility for the materials contained in any third party website referenced in this work.